RAND INTERNATIONAL

"The Project May Serve the Nation—But What About Us, Who Live Here?"

Villagers' Views of the Dawei Special Economic Zone, an Internationally Funded Infrastructure Project in Myanmar

Jonah Blank, Shira Efron, Katya Migacheva

For more information on this publication, visit www.rand.org/t/RR2416

Library of Congress Cataloging-in-Publication Data is available for this publication.
ISBN: 978-1-9774-0249-3

Published by the RAND Corporation, Santa Monica, Calif.
© Copyright 2019 RAND Corporation
RAND® is a registered trademark.

Cover: Prachatai/Flickr Creative Commons

Support RAND

Make a tax-deductible charitable contribution at
www.rand.org/giving/contribute

www.rand.org

Preface

A notable characteristic of Myanmar's political and economic reforms has been an influx of foreign investment, primarily from neighboring countries, in infrastructure and the extractive industries. One such project is the Dawei Special Economic Zone, which aims to link a key economic center in Myanmar with markets and suppliers in Thailand.

A key element that has been relatively absent from most assessments of Myanmar's economic engagement with outside investors has been the perspective of the local communities directly affected.

To assess the local community members' perceptions of foreign investment and its impact, RAND Corporation researchers collected primary data from a field study in the region. Findings from this study should be of interest to policymakers, development stakeholders, and academic researchers examining ways to boost Myanmar's economy and integration into the region.

RAND Ventures

The RAND Corporation is a research organization that develops solutions to public policy challenges to help make communities throughout the world safer and more secure, healthier and more prosperous. RAND is nonprofit, nonpartisan, and committed to the public interest.

RAND Ventures is a vehicle for investing in policy solutions. Philanthropic contributions support our ability to take the long view, tackle tough and often-controversial topics, and share our findings in innovative and compelling ways. RAND's research findings and recommendations are based on data and evidence and therefore do not necessarily reflect the policy preferences or interests of its clients, donors, or supporters.

Funding for this venture was provided by the generous contributions of the RAND Center for Asia Pacific Policy (CAPP) Advisory Board, and conducted within CAPP, part of International Programs at the RAND Corporation.

Support for this project is also provided, in part, by the income earned on client-funded research and from other donors.

Contents

Figures

Summary

Myanmar is a country in the midst of a historic transformation. In 2011, the country launched fundamental political and economic reforms aimed at increasing openness, empowerment, and inclusion, and the 2015 elections led the parliament to elect its first civilian state leader in decades. The country has been moving rapidly toward a market economy with a series of reforms indicating that its leadership is committed to integrating the country into the global economy. This commitment is also manifested in the many planned infrastructure and extractive industry development projects inside Myanmar, as well as projects that seek to connect the country to its neighbors.

To gain a better understanding of how foreign infrastructure investment in Myanmar may affect local communities, we conducted a survey of residents of communities near one such project—the Dawei Special Economic Zone (DSEZ). After a series of false starts beginning in 2008, the DSEZ project was transformed into a trilateral project led by the governments of Myanmar, Thailand, and Japan by 2015. When completed, the DSEZ is expected to become one of the largest industrial parks in Southeast Asia. We selected the DSEZ for study largely because it provided a way of examining the impact of foreign-funded economic development projects without involving two other key issues that often affect perceptions: attitudes toward China and the impact of government policies toward ethnic minorities.

Rather than looking at the DSEZ project solely from the top down (that is, from the perspective of central government policymakers and international investors), we sought to bring in the bottom-up views of the citizens most directly affected. As part of this research study conducted by the RAND Corporation, we polled 250 residents of nine villages near the DSEZ. Overall, we found that respondents expressed considerable skepticism about how the project would affect their lives. Most respondents saw outsiders (particularly foreigners) as the most likely beneficiaries of the DSEZ—and themselves as the parties most likely to suffer its ill effects. The problems of the project, however, were largely seen as solvable: Fewer than 9 percent wanted to terminate the DSEZ, and an overwhelming majority favored solutions (including higher compensation for confiscated land, hiring of more locals, and increased consultation) that are amenable to negotiation. If the government chooses to refocus efforts, it may have an opportunity to win the community's support. The message relayed by the survey data is one of alienation and skepticism but not necessarily outright opposition (at least not yet).

Given the scope of the project, the drastic impact it will have on the region, and the local population's sentiment that the central government bears ultimate responsibility for the DSEZ, Myanmar's government should ensure that the developers establish clear avenues for communication and cooperation with the local communities. This may be easier said than done.

The specific demands and proposals put forward by the communities may differ from those listed in this report. Thus, the meaningful involvement of the villagers themselves—and their genuine and trusted advocates—is fundamentally important for any stable and lasting solution. While consultations and a firm commitment to transparency may entail additional challenges, they will also ensure that the surrounding communities are more likely to act as supporters and facilitators of DSEZ investments and are willing to withstand some of the unanticipated problems and contribute to the project's success.

As Myanmar works to develop its infrastructure, it is in the ultimate interest of the central and regional governments to partner more effectively with local communities. To ensure the success of plans like the DSEZ, the people who are forced to alter their lives and livelihoods to accommodate such efforts must be—and must *feel* themselves to be—true beneficiaries of these projects.

Acknowledgments

We thank Saw Htay Wah for facilitating the field work in Myanmar and for enhancing our understanding of the complexities of Myanmar's social and economic challenges. We also thank our formal peer reviewers Nicholas Burger, senior economist at RAND, and Michael Kugelman, deputy director of the Asia Program and senior associate for South Asia at the Wilson Center. Finally, we thank the RAND Center for Asia Pacific Policy Advisory Board for funding this project and Scott Harold and Rafiq Dossani for their guidance and helpful feedback on earlier versions of this report.

Abbreviations

DDA   Dawei Development Association
DSEZ   Dawei Special Economic Zone
ITD   Italian-Thai Development

CHAPTER ONE

Introduction

Myanmar is a country in the midst of a historic transformation. In 2011, the country launched fundamental political and economic reforms aimed at increasing openness, empowerment, and inclusion. The November 8, 2015, elections marked a momentous event in Myanmar's history, when the opposition National League for Democracy swept into power, leading the parliament to elect its first civilian state leader in decades. Despite the persistence of such grave challenges as violence in minority ethnic areas, Myanmar has seen a dramatic increase in political and civil liberties in recent years. In parallel, the country has been moving rapidly toward a market economy with a series of reforms indicating that its leadership is committed to integrating the country into the global economy. This commitment is also manifested in the many planned infrastructure and extractive industry development projects inside Myanmar, as well as projects that seek to connect the country to its neighbors—some, but not all, of which are part of China's Belt and Road Initiative.

Through this study, we sought to provide context on infrastructure projects aimed at increasing Myanmar's economic engagement with the outside world: Rather than looking at these projects solely from the top down (that is, from the perspective of central government policymakers and international investors), we sought to bring in the views of the citizens most directly affected. As part of this research study conducted by the RAND Corporation, we polled 250 residents of nine villages near one particular infrastructure project and found that respondents expressed considerable skepticism about how the project would affect their lives. Yet, perhaps sensing the potential of the project to positively transform their lives and livelihoods, respondents preferred that project implementers consult those affected on how to improve the project rather than cancel it altogether. This suggests an important policy priority: Policymakers would be well advised to put more effort into consulting with local communities through all stages of development projects and pay greater attention to concerns, such as forced relocation, fair compensation, and equitable allotment of jobs and other resources.

Myanmar and Foreign Direct Investment

The second-largest country in Southeast Asia in terms of land area, Myanmar has one of the lowest population densities in the region, fertile lands, significant untapped agricultural potential, and a rich endowment of natural resources. It borders Bangladesh and India in the west and northwest, China in the north and northeast, and Laos and Thailand in the east and southeast. Its geographic location at the intersection of China and India—two of the world's most dynamic economies—makes it well positioned to resume its traditional role as a regional trading hub and a key supplier of minerals, natural gas, and agricultural produce.[1] To tap into this regional potential, Myanmar in 2011 began focusing on narrowing the significant gaps in its infrastructure development.[2] Indeed, in 2007, Myanmar was ranked 133

---

[1]   For a more detailed discussion, see Thant Myint-U, *Where China Meets India: Burma and the New Crossroads of Asia*, New York: Farrar, Straus and Giroux, 2011.

[2]   Myanmar's economic and political reforms had their origin in the Saffron Revolution of August–October 2007. In May 2008—with its legitimacy weakened by an ineffective response to Cyclone Nargis, a disaster that resulted in 138,000 deaths—Myanmar's military junta held a constitutional referendum. In 2010, it held an election (boycotted by popular democratic leader Aung San Suu Kyi), which did little to restore public confidence. On November 13, 2010, Aung San Suu Kyi was released from house arrest. In 2011, the military junta instituted a program of economic liberalization, perhaps thinking that economic reforms might be de-coupled from political liberalization. In 2015, the military-led government permitted elections, which were considered generally free and fair and which resulted in the political victory of Aung San Suu Kyi's party, the National League of Democracy.

out of 155 in the World Bank's Logistics Performance Index, which is considered a proxy on the state of transport infrastructure. By 2016, four years after initiating an infrastructure development program, the nation had climbed 20 places to rank at 113 among nations in the index.[3] This progress, however limited, shows the potential for change and the importance of foreign direct investment to Myanmar and its neighbors.

For decades, a limited set of foreign investors have funded projects in Myanmar, particularly those in the extractive resource industries. One of the highest profile of these was a 1990s pipeline proposal by the U.S. oil company Unocal, but because of concerns about the potential for forced labor and other human rights abuses, the project collapsed before work could begin. During the 1990s and beyond, sanctions imposed on Myanmar by the United States and European nations ensured that most projects in the country would be funded by China. However, since the Barack Obama administration dropped most of these economic sanctions, the number of projects—and of nations supporting these efforts—has exploded. Many of these are still focused on extractive industries, but many others are aimed at improving land connectivity and transportation links. The government of Myanmar is relying on such foreign investment to boost the nation's economic development and connectivity to its neighbors. But many of the same questions that led to sanctions in the 1990s remain unanswered: Will these projects genuinely benefit the local communities? Will projects result in forced labor, involuntary land confiscation, or other violations of either human or civil rights?[4]

---

[3] World Bank, "Country Score Card: Myanmar 2014," Logistics Performance Index, 2014.

[4] Advocacy organizations asking these questions include the Urban Climate Resilience in Southeast Asia Partnership. For an articulation of this group's critique, see Danny Marks and Tammy Chou, "It's Time to Scrap the Dawei Special Economic Zone," *Frontier Myanmar*, August 29, 2017. For a more academic discussion of these issues, see S. Chantavanich and P. Vungsiriphisal, "Myanmar Migrants to Thailand: Economic Analysis and Implications to Myanmar Development," in Hank Lim and Yasuhiro Yamada, eds., *Economic Reforms in Myanmar: Pathways and Prospects*, Bangkok: Bangkok Research Center, Research Report No. 10, IDE-JETRO, 2013; and Myat Thein, *Economic Development of Myanmar*, Singapore: Institute of Southeast Asian Studies, 2004, pp. 175–235.

Dawei Special Economic Zone

To gain a better understanding of how foreign infrastructure investment in Myanmar may affect local communities, we conducted a survey of residents of communities near one such project—the Dawei Special Economic Zone (DSEZ). After a series of false starts beginning in 2008, the DSEZ project was transformed into a trilateral project led by the governments of Myanmar, Thailand, and Japan by 2015. When completed, the DSEZ is expected to become one of the largest industrial parks in Southeast Asia.[5] We selected the DSEZ for study largely because it provided a way of examining the impact of foreign-funded economic development projects without involving two other key issues that often affect perceptions: attitudes toward China and the impact of government policies toward ethnic minorities.

Perceptions about the DSEZ are not tangled up in popular perceptions about China for a simple reason: The DSEZ is a Thai-Japanese venture rather than a Chinese one; anti-Chinese sentiments stirred up by resource-extraction projects elsewhere in Myanmar have little direct impact here. Likewise, the project is not directly affected by the ethnic unrest and counterinsurgency campaigns being conducted elsewhere in the nation. The local population in Dawei is largely Bamar and Tavoy—that is, it belongs to ethnic groups that constitute nearly two-thirds of the nation's population.[6] The often-brutal counterinsurgency campaigns that complicate projects in areas with large populations of ethnic minorities, such as Shan, Mon, and Karen, do not operate in Dawei. The biggest problem facing Myanmar—and potential foreign investors in Myanmar—today is the ethnic cleansing campaign against the nation's Rohingya population; at the time of this writing, approximately 700,000 Rohingyas, out of a population estimated to number

---

[5] "Thailand, Myanmar to Revive South-East Asia's Largest Industrial Zone in 2015," *Straits Times*, December 4, 2014.

[6] The Bamar constitute the bulk of this two-thirds; the Tavoy are a smaller related group. Of the 250 survey respondents, 140 were Tavoy and 107 were Bamar.

about 1 million,[7] have been driven into exile in neighboring Bangladesh. For any project operating in Rakhine State, this event would be such a dominant fact that it would overshadow any other research questions. Given the ethnic composition of the local population in Dawei, however, this topic was not a significant factor in the research.

The goal of this research project was to assess the impact—economic, political, social, and cultural—of the DSEZ on the local community, as perceived by the community members themselves. In the following chapters, we provide background information on the evolution of the DSEZ since its inception in 2008, followed by a description of the study we undertook to examine the project's impact on the well-being of local communities—as described by the respondents. We conclude with a summary of our observations and recommendations for policymakers for the future development of this project. We also discuss how an understanding of local populations' perceptions about this project and its current and future impact may give insights into the opportunities and challenges that other Myanmar infrastructure projects may face in the years ahead.

---

[7] Ben Otto, "Rohingya Camps in Bangladesh Start to Look Permanent," *Wall Street Journal*, April 3, 2018.

CHAPTER TWO

Background: Ups and Downs in the Evolution of the Dawei Special Economic Zone

Between the time it gained its independence from Great Britain in 1948 and the beginning of economic reforms in 2011, Myanmar's economy had been largely stagnant. Following Ne Win's accession to power in 1962, the nation embarked on a program termed the Burmese Way to Socialism, which resulted in resource-rich Myanmar dropping in 1987 to the tier classified by the United Nations and other international institutions as a *least developed country*. Much of the nation's economy throughout the second half of the 20th century was centered around agriculture (although not at levels sufficient for export) and extraction of natural resources (much of it illicit—such as illegal logging and unregulated mining for gemstones). As is common in economies dominated by illicit trade, much of the profit was siphoned off by corruption before it could reach the large mass of the citizenry. What little above-board trade Myanmar had was largely with China and, to some degree, with its immediate neighbors Thailand and Laos.

A visitor returning to Myanmar not long after the 2011 reforms would have found a great deal changed. The financial center of Yangon, which had been a sleepy backwater city until well after the turn of the 21st century, was newly bustling with trade and traffic jams. Construction sites were everywhere. The change was spurred both by the genuine economic reform agenda of the Burmese government and by a rapid international re-engagement led by the United States; several European nations; and such key Asian players as Thailand, Singapore, Japan, and South Korea. In the space of half a decade, Myanmar had begun making real progress toward eventually joining the ranks of the "four Asian tigers" (i.e., the formidable economies of Hong Kong, Singapore, South Korea, and Taiwan).[1]

The DSEZ is located in Dawei, the capital of the Tanintharyi Region along the Thai-Myanmar peninsula. It extends over some 200 km^2 and is home to a pristine beach. Nevertheless, its designers intend to (1) develop it as a deep-sea port and a petrochemical and heavy industry hub and (2) connect it to the rest of the country via modern road and rail links.[2] The DSEZ was launched in 2008 with a memorandum of understanding signed by Thailand and Myanmar. At an estimated development price tag of $8 billion, it is one of three special economic zones in Myanmar designed to attract foreign direct investment through the use of unprecedented tax exemptions and other incentives.[3] Once completed, the DSEZ is expected to be the largest industrial zone in Southeast Asia.[4] The deep-sea port and improved transport links to Thailand were seen as particularly attractive to foreign investors, but the planned road and rail links could ultimately connect the area to Thailand, Cambodia, and all the way to Vietnam.[5]

Initially, the DSEZ was managed by a private Thailand-based firm, Italian-Thai Development (ITD). Although the project launched with the promise of mobilizing "millions of Burmese" (in the words of ITD president Premchai Karnasuta), fears that the best interests of

---

[1]   For discussion of Myanmar's economic engagement with India—which has high hopes of rivaling China as an economic partner and major developer of infrastructure—see Jonah Blank, Jennifer D. P. Moroney, Angel Rabasa, and Bonny Lin, *Look East, Cross Black Waters: India's Interest in Southeast Asia*, Santa Monica, Calif.: RAND Corporation, RR-1021-AF, 2015, pp. 96–101; and Jonah Blank, "India's Engagement with Myanmar: Regional Security Implications of Acting East Slowly," in Karen Stoll Farrell and Šumit Ganguly, eds., *Heading East: Security, Trade, and Environment Between India and Southeast Asia*, New Delhi: Oxford University Press, 2016, pp. 75–79.

[2]   Theingi Htun, "Dawei SEZ Project Sparks Hopes and Worries," *Mizzima*, January 25, 2016.

[3]   Zaw Aung, "Dawei Special Economic Zone: Its Prospects and Challenges," paper presented at the 4th International Conference on Human Rights and Human Development, Chulalongkorn University, Thailand, August 18–19, 2011.

[4]   "Thailand, Myanmar to Revive South-East Asia's Largest Industrial Zone in 2015," 2014.

[5]   Larry Jagan, "Myanmar Renews SEZ Push," *Bangkok Post*, October 2, 2017.

the citizens of Myanmar would not be sufficiently prioritized arose early on. The 2010 press accounts highlighted concerns that the DSEZ would just be "a cheap and convenient way to export [Thailand's] dirty refineries across the border," where antipollution regulations would not apply.[6] The site of the project likewise seemed to benefit Thailand more than Myanmar: The roads and seaport proposed at Dawei would provide Thailand with desirable maritime access routes to India, the Middle East, Europe, and Africa—but a better site for a seaport from Myanmar's perspective would have been located closer to the country's industrial base.[7]

In addition, the project faced difficulties in drawing investment and has faced strong opposition from civil society organizations.[8] Residents of villages in the DSEZ have complained about being forced to evacuate their homes without proper compensation and about the DSEZ delivering more benefit to foreign investors than to the local community. In 2013, Dawei villagers and civil society groups lodged an official complaint to Thailand's National Human Rights Commission, which has been investigating; Thailand has vowed to comply with the United Nations' guiding principles on human rights.[9] Given the human rights complaints leveled against Thailand's own government (particularly those stemming from the 2014 military coup d'état), it is possible that the military junta leading Thailand had little incentive to devote much attention to human rights concerns in other nations.

Progress in moving from the conceptual stage to concrete action was slow, and the political transition of Myanmar's national government to greater civilian rule in 2015 cast the future of the DSEZ (along with most projects negotiated during the period of military rule) into doubt.[10] Since that time, however, the project has been transformed

---

[6] "An Industrial Project That Could Change Myanmar," *International Herald Tribune: The Global Edition of the New York Times,* November 26, 2010.

[7] Panu Wongcha-um, "Split Visions of Dawei's Future as Thailand, Myanmar Restart Special Economic Zone Project," *Channel News Asia*, May 25, 2017.

[8] Panu, 2017; Marks and Chou, 2017.

[9] Panu, 2017.

[10] Panu, 2017.

into a trilateral cooperation among the governments of Myanmar, Thailand, and Japan, with the three countries having equal shares in the project. If completed according to plan (and some analysts consider the plan overly optimistic[11]), the project will include a two-way highway from the economic zone to the Myanmar-Thai border at Thi Khi, a deepwater port, a power plant, landline telecom service, a liquefied natural gas terminal, and what has been billed as one of the largest industrial parks in Southeast Asia.[12] By late September 2017, two task forces had been set up to review and facilitate the DSEZ development. One of them is mandated with assessing the project's progress and the other with addressing time frame and finance issues.

In light of renewed investment in the project, representatives of civil society groups, such as the Myanmar Special Economic Zone Watch, have again started calling for compliance with environmental protection laws and for greater transparency to ensure project acceptance by the local community.[13] This attention by nongovernmental organizations and community groups can be seen as part of a larger global context in which grassroots activists are pitted against international commercial concerns. Whenever a project brings relocation, job competition, or adverse environmental impacts to a community, questions arise about who the real beneficiaries of such a project will be: Are any adverse impacts outweighed by the economic opportunities provided? Is the compensation that is offered by the company or the government (if any) truly proportionate to the costs incurred by the local population? Can harms that are not easily quantifiable (such as loss of community cohesion or erosion of traditional cultural or religious practices) ever be adequately mitigated? Who is best placed to serve as the legitimate voice of society—particularly when companies may seek to co-opt a stratum of the local elite, perhaps at the expense of the larger community? International nongovernmental organizations,

---

[11] Marks and Chou, 2017.

[12] Brennan O'Connor, "Myanmar: The Dawei Special Economic Zone: Amid Delays, Local Opposition to the Project Is Growing," *The Diplomat*, April 11, 2016.

[13] Su Phyo Win, "Two New Taskforces to Monitor and Facilitate Dawei SEZ," *Myanmar Times*, September 28, 2017.

including Oxfam and Human Rights Watch, have addressed such concerns from an advocacy standpoint.[14] Scholars and other writers who have examined these and related questions from a nonadvocacy standpoint include, among others, Paul Roberts, Fred Pearce, Michael Kugelman, and Susan Levenstein.[15]

---

[14] Examples include B. Zegema, *Land and Power: The Growing Scandal Surrounding the New Wave of Investments in Land*, Oxford, UK: Oxfam International, Oxfam Briefing Paper 151, September 22, 2001; K. Geary, *"Our Land, Our Lives": Time Out on the Global Land Rush*, Oxford, UK: Oxfam International, Briefing Note, October 2012; and, within Myanmar itself, Human Rights Watch, *"The Farmer Becomes the Criminal": Land Confiscation in Burma's Karen State*, New York, November 2016.

[15] Paul Roberts, *The End of Food: The Coming Crisis in the World Food Industry*, New York: Mariner Books, 2009; Fred Pearce, *The Land Grabbers: The New Fight over Who Owns the Earth*, Boston, Mass.: Beacon Press, 2012; and Michael Kugelman and Susan L. Levenstein, eds., *The Global Farms Race: Land Grabs, Agricultural Investment, and the Scramble for Food Security*, Washington, D.C.: Island Press, 2013, Chapters 1, 4, and 12.

CHAPTER THREE

Research Objective and Methodology

Research Objective

The goal of this study is to understand how the local community in the DSEZ perceives the project. This is an important question both from an economic perspective (because resistance from civil society is often cited as one of the reasons for the DSEZ's slow progress) and from a policy perspective (that is, how policymakers in the government of Myanmar can learn from this experience). The only substantive prior survey on this topic was conducted by the Dawei Development Association (DDA), a local grassroots communal rights organization, which published its findings in December 2013.[1] In its report, DDA selected 20 villages determined to face likely impacts from the DSEZ and reported responses from inhabitants flagging significant potential for a wide range of direct and indirect harms to the local population. DDA argued the following:

- All of the villages, even before the project had truly gotten underway, were already suffering adverse impacts.
- As the project progressed, far more people were likely to suffer adverse impacts to their livelihoods, environment, and health.
- The DSEZ managers, and the governments of Myanmar and Thailand, had failed to provide adequate information to, or consult with, the communities affected.

---

[1] DDA, *Voices from the Ground: Concerns over the Dawei Special Economic Zone and Related Projects*, Dawei, Myanmar, September 2014.

- The process for compensating villagers for lost land or livelihoods was "deeply flawed."
- "Systemic failures in the initial implementation of the DSEZ project [were] causing hardship for affected people."[2]

In this study, we seek to assess the local community's view of the DSEZ now that the project has moved from its initial phases to a stage in which direct impacts are more easily visible. This study builds on and supplements DDA's research in several important ways. First, we provide an updated picture of the project's impact: The original data for this study were collected four years more recently than DDA's survey data (June–July 2017, compared with September 2013) and therefore provide the opportunity to see whether villagers' initial concerns have been borne out by subsequent developments. Second, we collected substantial original microdata that helped us conduct different types of richer and more-nuanced analysis of the DSEZ than might have been possible without such enumeration details.[3] Third, and perhaps most importantly, the RAND Corporation's status as a nonpartisan research organization provides an outlook different from that of the prior study. DDA is an advocacy group, and its findings were presented in that context;[4] this institutional mission in no way detracts from the quality or importance of the study, but it may have shaped the context in which the study was received. Policymakers, whether in Myanmar, Thailand, or the business community, often dismiss or downplay the findings of studies generated by advocacy groups. In some cases, such an attitude stems from a sincere doubt

---

[2]   DDA, 2014, p. 6.

[3]   Our survey contained rich data about each individual respondent's ethnic background, educational level, and other basic demographic information rather than such data in the aggregate. In addition, our collection and analysis were governed by RAND's strict protocol on protection of human subjects' data. This protocol requires considerably more time and systemic methods of secure data management than many other survey techniques, and it therefore permits a closer-grained analysis without jeopardizing individuals' privacy or safety.

[4]   For example, the DDA study concludes with an open letter of petition for redress from the National Human Rights Commission of Thailand (DDA, 2014, Annex II, pp. 85–86).

about the credibility of such studies, while, in others, it may be the result merely of self-interest. Regardless of the motive for such dismissal, a study by researchers from an institution like RAND—firmly committed to scholarship without competing financial or ideological interests—could serve to either credibly validate or recalibrate the findings of the advocacy group.

As it turns out, this study does both. It recalibrates some of the DDA findings, which place more focus on the negative than the positive impressions of the project.[5] More often, however, this study serves to validate and reinforce some of the key points raised by the villagers surveyed by DDA: Four years after the DDA team conducted its work, respondents to the RAND survey expressed many of the same fears, concerns, and discontents. These were notably focused on perceived inadequate information, consultation, and compensation for lost land and livelihoods.

Methodology

To assess how people in the villages within the DSEZ viewed the project and its past, current, and future impacts, we designed a survey that contained both multiple-choice and open-ended questions. The survey was then translated from English into Burmese and vetted by native Burmese speakers.

Through recommendations by local community leaders, we recruited 27 native Burmese interviewers from the Dawei region and trained them to conduct the survey. The interviewers were instructed to knock on the door of every fourth house in each village and ask an adult in the house to answer the questions on the survey. The interviewers were instructed to alternate asking a male or a female member of the household to answer the survey. Once participants agreed to take part in the survey, they were informed that their participation

---

[5] This recalibration may be due to the passage of time; perhaps villagers were less pessimistic now that they have had four additional years to see how the DSEZ has progressed. It is also possible that the difference is due to the different institutional missions and purposes of DDA and RAND.

was completely voluntary and confidential and that they could stop answering questions at any time. Altogether, 250 participants across nine villages completed the survey (see Figure 3.1). This represents a response rate of approximately 90 percent.

The interviewers read the questions to the participants, offered response options (where relevant), and recorded participants' responses. Participants' names were not recorded on the surveys; however, the interviewers observed or requested and then noted each participant's age, sex, level of education, and ethnicity. Upon the completion of data collection, participants' responses were translated into English, and we analyzed the results.

Figure 3.1
Map of Villages Surveyed

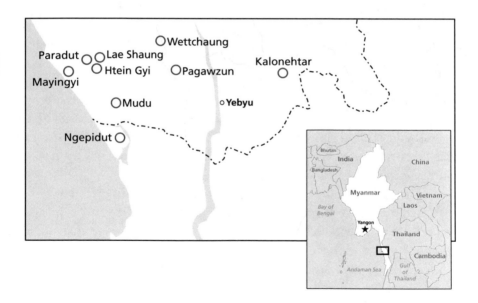

CHAPTER FOUR

Findings: Local Community Views on the Dawei Special Economic Zone

As described earlier, 250 people agreed to respond to the survey, and the enumeration details of the survey set merit a brief discussion.

The survey team sought a roughly equal gender distribution among respondents and ended up with a set that was 55 percent female. The respondents tilted toward the older side of the age spectrum: Only 12 percent were under age 40, with a plurality (42 percent) between ages 51 and 64, nearly another quarter (24 percent) aged 65 or older, and 22 percent between ages 40 and 50. Participants were recruited from nine villages, with the largest segment from Lae Shaung (24 percent); the smallest segments from Ngepidut (4 percent) and Mayingyi (6 percent); and the remaining two-thirds of respondents divided among Mudu (14 percent), Htein Gyi (13 percent), Paradut (12 percent), Pagawzun (12 percent), Wettchaung (8 percent), and Kalonehtar (8 percent).[1] More than half of the participants identified their ethnicity as Tavoy (56 percent), while the rest self-identified as Bamar (42 percent) or "other" (2 percent).

Half of the respondents had received an elementary school education (Grades 1–4), one-fifth had attended middle school (Grades 5–8), 9 percent had graduated from high school, and 4 percent had earned a college degree; 18 percent had no formal education. More than three-quarters (77 percent) of the participants were natives of the villages in which they were surveyed.

---

[1] Throughout the report, we have rounded percentages to the nearest whole number, so these values might not always sum exactly to 100.

The respondents were overwhelmingly on the lower end of the income scale. Nearly 60 percent of participants reported their annual income as falling into the lowest possible bracket: between 100,000 and 1.8 million kyat. The upper end of this bracket represents a figure only about 40-percent higher than the nation's nominal minimum wage, and its lower end represents virtually no cash income at all. Most of the other respondents (31 percent of all respondents) reported annual incomes between 1.8 million and 3.6 million kyat. Even the high end of this bracket is equivalent to barely one-third of the nation's estimated gross domestic product per capita.[2]

More than half of the respondents (58 percent) described themselves as unfamiliar with the project, while approximately 40 percent said that they were familiar with it to some degree (Figure 4.1).[3] This raises an important methodological question about whether to examine the opinions of all respondents surveyed or only of those who described themselves as familiar with the project. We decided that a more accurate picture would be provided by including the respondents who described themselves as unfamiliar rather than excluding them from the sample set. The rationale for inclusion is as follows:

- The survey is a measure of the opinions of the community, not of its knowledge (or of the opinions only of its most knowledgeable members). The support or opposition to any development project is not limited to members who are familiar with its details; indeed, political support or opposition is sometimes driven by the least-informed community members.

---

[2]   At the time of writing, 100,000 kyat was approximately $63, 1.8 million kyat was $1,135, and 3.6 million kyat was $2,270 (all dollars in 2018 U.S. dollars) (Xe, "Currency Converter," web tool, accessed November 6, 2018). Two years before the survey was conducted, Myanmar instituted a national minimum wage of 3,600 kyat per day, or roughly $804 per year (assuming a standard-for-Myanmar six-day workweek) ("Myanmar Sets $2.80 Daily Minimum Wage in Bid to Boost Investment," Reuters, August 29, 2015). The gross domestic product per capita in the year that survey data were collected (2017) was estimated by the Central Intelligence Agency at $6,200 (Central Intelligence Agency, *The World Factbook: Burma*, accessed November 6, 2018).

[3]   The methodological questions raised by the high response rate of "not at all familiar" are addressed in the appendix.

Figure 4.1
Are You Familiar with the Dawei Project?

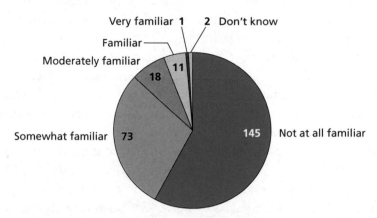

NOTES: For this figure and all remaining figures in this report and its appendix, the numbers presented count the number of survey respondents selecting that answer choice. (Figure 4.10, which reports the percentage of respondents, is the one exception.)

- A survey respondent's self-description as familiar or unfamiliar may have had little to do with his or her actual level of knowledge. Some community members—particularly in a society like Myanmar's in which honest articulation of opinions can be a hazardous choice—may have wildly varying degrees of comfort in putting themselves forward as reliable voices.
- Those who described themselves as unfamiliar with the project nonetheless expressed very definite opinions about it. A close look at the data provided by respondents who described themselves as not familiar tracked quite closely with the sentiments of those who expressed much greater familiarity.

A more complete discussion, along with analysis of the data from "not at all familiar" and more-familiar respondents, is provided in the appendix to this report.

Of the sizable minority of respondents who did see a significant impact from the DSEZ (e.g., 43 percent when asked how the project affected their neighbors' or the community's employment; see Figure 4.2), more saw it as negative than positive. More than twice as many respondents saw a negative impact than a positive one in the areas of family employment, family health, and health of the community (Figure 4.2 and Figure 4.3). High school graduates were more likely than lower-educated respondents to see the project as harming their or their community's health. This may be due to concerns about the adverse health impacts of similar projects in Thailand, particularly those involving storage or shipment of petrochemicals and other hazardous materials. News reports describing these hazards circulated in some outlets in Myanmar, which may also account for the higher level of health concerns expressed by better-educated respondents (i.e., those more likely to have read accounts in local newspapers or online regional websites).[4]

Figure 4.2
How Has the Dawei Project Affected the Local Employment Situation?

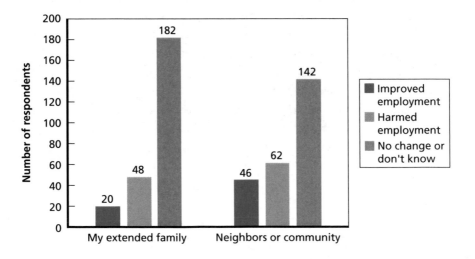

4   Such reports include Ei Ei Toe Lwin, "Dawei SEZ Sparks Concern amid Promises," *Myanmar Times*, December 3, 2012; Kyaw Hsu Mon, "In Dawei, ITD Projects Suspended, Not Terminated: Minister," *The Irrawaddy*, December 3, 2013; Ei Ei Toe Lwin, "Civil Soci-

Figure 4.3
How Has the Project Affected Local Health Outcomes?

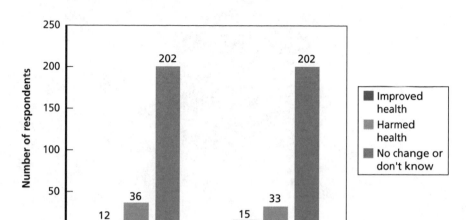

Respondents tended to describe a system in which they felt that they had limited control over their fates. While two-thirds felt that they could express grievances, such as concerns about health and employment, without fear (Figure 4.4), only one-fifth of the survey respondents felt that authorities had heard and addressed these grievances (Figure 4.5).

Just less than one-third of respondents felt that their community had an advocate (such as a civil society organization) representing their interests (Figure 4.6), and, of this group, barely 10 percent expressed confidence in the advocate (Figure 4.7).

ety Group Calls for Freeze on Dawei Economic Zone," *Myanmar Times*, October 13, 2014; and Jason Szep and Amy Sawitta Lefevre, "Japan, Thailand Race to Rescue Myanmar's Struggling Dawei," Reuters, September 21, 2012.

Figure 4.4
Can You Express Grievances Without Fear?

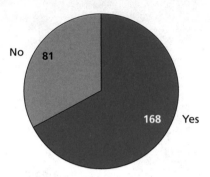

NOTE: One respondent did not answer this question.

Figure 4.5
Have Your Grievances Been Heard and Addressed?

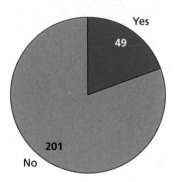

Figure 4.6
Do Local People Have Advocates?

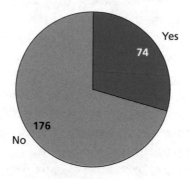

Figure 4.7
If You Do Have Advocates, Do You Have Confidence in Them?

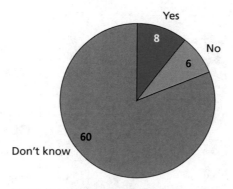

NOTE: This question was asked only of respondents who answered "yes" to the question in Figure 4.6.

Despite this lack of agency and social trust in representative government, however, only one-fifth of respondents said that the Myanmar authorities had failed to address their concerns or the concerns of their community; more than one-third felt that the authorities had addressed concerns fairly, while a plurality (44 percent) expressed no opinion or lack of certainty that grievances were sufficiently addressed (Figure 4.8).[5]

With respect to the employment consequences of the DSEZ, nearly half of respondents felt that it was difficult to get a job on the project, compared with only 13 percent who thought it was easy. Only 34 respondents—14 percent of the pool—had worked on the project, even for a period of weeks or months (Figure 4.9).

Figure 4.8
Have the Myanmar Authorities Addressed Your or Your Community's Concerns?

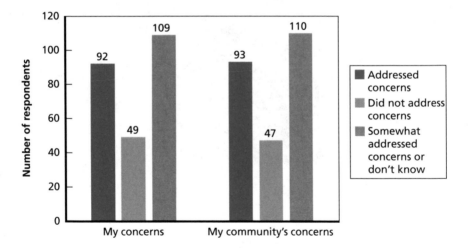

---

[5]   In their unstructured comments, respondents did not address the discrepancy between their lack of confidence in the process and their relatively muted criticism of the actual impact. One possible explanation is that a majority of respondents were apprehensive about the project's potential future impact and felt alienated from the decisionmaking process but had not seen their personal concerns rebuffed by project authorities.

Figure 4.9
Have You Worked on the
Dawei Project?

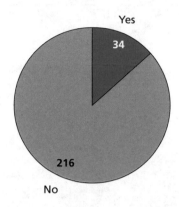

Of these 34 respondents, only four (12 percent) found it easy to get a project job, and most of the others judged it to be difficult. A plurality of project workers had no strong opinion about work conditions or pay. Among those who did express positive or negative assessments, nearly twice as many judged working conditions to be good as judged them to be poor—but nearly three times as many found the pay unfair as found it fair. Respondents who had graduated high school were far more likely to see pay as unfair (87.5 percent) than were those with only a primary school education (about 20 percent) (Figure 4.10). This suggests that the pay scales for supervisory jobs or other posts requiring some education were not adequately compensated, that better-educated respondents were taking menial rather than administrative jobs, or that better-educated responders were better equipped to recognize the unfair pay patterns.

Respondents also tended to feel that jobs at the DSEZ project were primarily going to people outside the community (Figure 4.11). A plurality (41 percent) felt that jobs were primarily going to foreigners (23 percent) and workers from other parts of Myanmar (18 percent). Another 34 percent felt that these groups and locals were all getting employment on equal terms—that is, locals were getting one-third of the available posts. Only 13 percent saw the jobs as going primarily to locals.

Figure 4.10
Perceived Fairness of Compensation, by Highest Completed Education Level

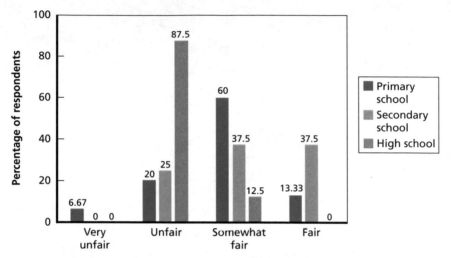

NOTE: This question was asked only of respondents who answered "yes" to the question in Figure 4.9.

Figure 4.11
Where Do Project Workers Come From?

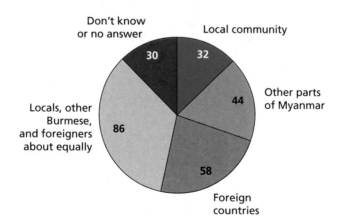

Respondents overwhelmingly believed that the foreign workers on the Dawei project were coming from Thailand (89 percent) (Figure 4.12). These responses may have been referring to manual labor positions rather than supervisory ones. Respondents seemed to be less certain about the administrative positions: Responses that most jobs were going to workers from Japan (the second-highest nation listed, at 3 percent); from China (2 percent—uninvolved in this project, but active in many others); and from Singapore, India, and the United States (all uninvolved in the Dawei project) likely were referring to foreign administrators with whom most of the locals would have had little contact.

Figure 4.12
Where Do the Foreign Workers Employed on the Dawei Project Come From?

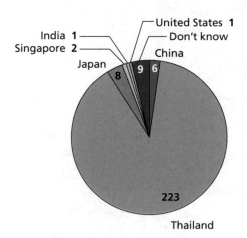

The issue of relocation and appropriation of land is perhaps the sorest point for the local community, although, for most respondents, it is more of a fear for the future than a complaint about the present. Only four respondents (less than 2 percent) had been relocated, and an additional 31 (12 percent) had been asked to relocate but had refused; of these, about half had refused for lack of sufficient compensation, and the other half refused for noneconomic reasons (reluctance to leave their community, for example). Thirty-three respondents (13 percent) reported that they had given up their farmland, while another 20 (8 percent) had refused to do so.

Of the 33 respondents who gave up their farmland, only five felt that they had received fair compensation. Thirteen felt that their compensation had been unfair, and 15 reported receiving no compensation at all (Figure 4.13).

Only three of the 33 respondents reported that their economic situation had improved since they gave up their land. Most (61 percent) reported that their financial condition had worsened, and the remainder reported no significant change (Figure 4.14).

Figure 4.13
Have You Been Fairly Compensated for Loss of Farmland?

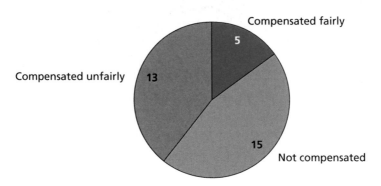

NOTE: This question was asked only of respondents who reported that they had given up their farmland.

Figure 4.14
Since Giving Up Your Farmland, How Has Your
Economic Situation Changed?

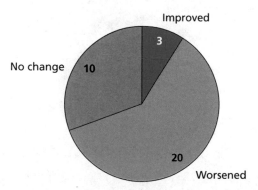

NOTE: This question was asked only of respondents
who reported that they had given up their farmland.

Reports of gross abuse, however, were rare (see Figure 4.15).[6] Only seven respondents (3 percent) reported forced labor, physical abuse, or intimidation. A range of the comments provided by the respondents describing why they moved off their land included the following (we list how we categorized each response in parentheses):

- "Forced to sign a document by village chief" (forced labor).
- "Forced into accepting a deal" (forced labor).
- "Forced to give away our produce" (forced labor and physical abuse).
- "I wasn't allowed by village head to repair my house" (intimidation).
- "Village administrator and ITD threatened villagers" (intimidation).

---

6   U.S. law states that

the term "gross violations of internationally recognized human rights" includes torture or cruel, inhuman, or degrading treatment or punishment, prolonged detention without charges and trial, causing the disappearance of persons by the abduction and clandestine detention of those persons, and other flagrant denial of the right to life, liberty, or the security of the person. (United States Code, Title 22, Chapter 32, Section 2304, Human Rights and Security Assistance)

**Figure 4.15
Experience of Hardship Due to the Project**

- "Legal case involving land dispute, and was imprisoned 2 months" (intimidation).
- "We are not permitted to cultivate our land" (intimidation).

It is possible that additional cases of abuse were unreported, but the descriptions provided by these seven seem to suggest that instances of abuse are episodic rather than widespread and pervasive.

The most common experience of direct harm from the project cited by respondents was food insecurity. Thirteen respondents said that they had suffered from food insecurity, and selected comments include the following:

- "We have to buy rice due to damage to our land."
- "Our farmland was confiscated."
- "Household experiences food shortage many times."
- "We experience shortage of food supply."
- "We can no longer harvest our rich fields."
- "Flooding causes damage to our farmlands."
- "We have to depend on borrowed farmland."
- "We gave up our farmland."

CHAPTER FIVE

Expectations for the Future

Nearly four times as many respondents expected that they personally would be hurt by the project as felt that they would be helped, and more than twice as many felt that their community would be harmed as felt that it would be helped (Figure 5.1); about half of respondents either expected no personal impact or did not know what to expect. By contrast, more than ten times as many respondents thought that the government of Myanmar would be helped by the project as felt that it would be harmed. Respondents saw the central government, along with foreign developers and local contractors, as the most likely to experience a positive impact. For the Dawei region—that is, the area midway between the local and the national level—the prediction was split almost evenly, with a slight tilt toward a positive impact.

When the question was posed in a slightly (but meaningfully) different way, respondents offered somewhat different replies. Instead of asking respondents whether they expected the project to bring benefit or harm, the interviewers asked which group respondents thought would benefit the most and which would be harmed the most. When phrased this way, more than half (53 percent) of respondents listed the local community as the entity most harmed (Figure 5.2). Only 5 percent of respondents rated their household or community as the most likely beneficiary of the project (Figure 5.3). This follows the trendline of the previous question but provides a more pessimistic assessment.

An even more noteworthy divergence is in respondents' predictions about the impact on the government of Myanmar. Under this phrasing, nearly one-fifth of respondents cited the government in

Figure 5.1
Expectations for Project Impact

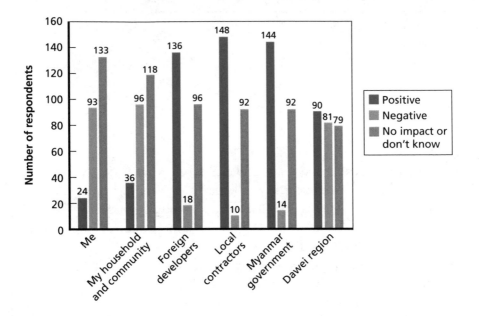

Figure 5.2
Who Will Be Harmed Most by the Dawei Project?

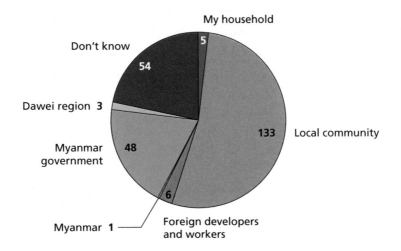

Figure 5.3
Who Will Benefit Most from the Dawei Project?

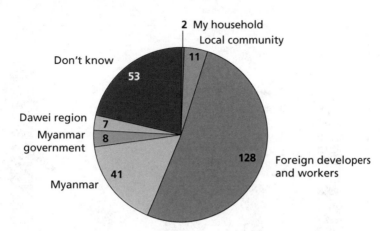

Naypyidaw as the entity most harmed by the project, and only 3 percent listed it as the most likely beneficiary. (Foreign developers were cited as the primary beneficiary by a majority of respondents, and the Dawei region was not seen by many respondents as either the key victim or beneficiary).[1]

The main hopes for the DSEZ project were almost entirely economic: Some respondents cited their hopes as general economic improvement, and some specified the potential for future employment. The concerns and fears, however, were primarily outside of the economic arena. Just 10 percent of respondents cited compensation as their primary concern (Figure 5.4). This may indicate that even compensation for the economic value of confiscated land and lost livelihood would not allay community misgivings about loss of such intangible assets as heritage, family ties, and social cohesion. More respondents cited concerns about challenges to culture or heritage (29) than cited con-

---

[1] It is possible that the divergence in the results is due to differences in the question structure: The phrasing of the second question (whose responses are reported in Figures 5.2 and 5.3) separated the "Myanmar government" from "Myanmar" and had only two local or personal response categories ("my household" and "local community") rather than three ("me," "my household," and "my [or local] community," the last two of which are combined in Figure 5.1).

Figure 5.4
Respondents' Biggest Concerns About the Project

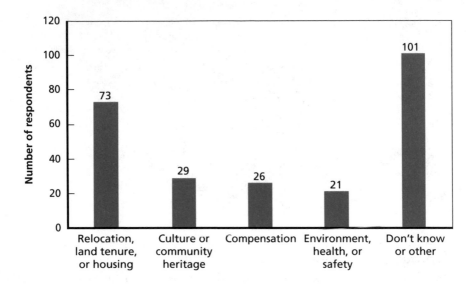

cerns about compensation (26), and nearly as many cited fears about the impact on the community's environment, health, or safety (21). By far the greatest concern, however, was the prospect of relocation (along with the intertwined issues of land tenure and housing): Nearly as many respondents cited this set of issues as their main concern (73) as cited the other three sets of issues combined (76 total for questions related to compensation, culture, and the environment).

Relocation was a sore point for a strong plurality of respondents, particularly for those who had the lowest levels of education (46 percent of whom cited this as their key concern). Respondents overwhelmingly described themselves as not at all prepared for relocation (82 percent) (Figure 5.5) or for the prospect of giving up their farmland (71 percent) (Figure 5.6).

Despite these concerns, respondents were more optimistic about the project's long-term impact than about its effects in the short term. Slightly more respondents expected benefits than expected harm in the future for their own families and communities, and a plurality of

Figure 5.5
How Prepared Would You Be to Relocate?

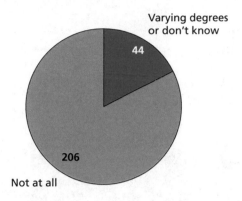

Figure 5.6
How Prepared Would You Be to Give Up Your Farmland?

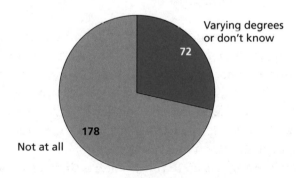

respondents saw the project as benefiting Myanmar as a whole in the future (Figure 5.7).[2]

Just as most respondents saw the nation of Myanmar as more likely to benefit from the project than the local community was, a majority (55 percent) of respondents saw the government of Myanmar

---

[2]   It is noteworthy that there was no significant difference in this response between the two major ethnic groups represented in our sample, Tavoy and Bamar.

Figure 5.7
How Do You Think the Project Will Benefit Your Family, the Local Community, and Myanmar in the Long Term?

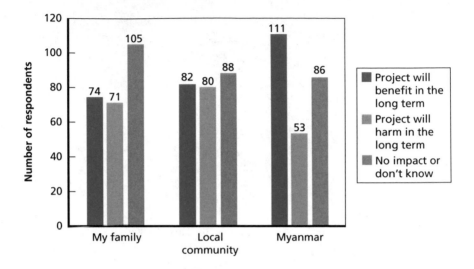

as bearing the primary responsibility and accountability for the project's impact (Figure 5.8). Developers and investors together were cited by 11 percent of respondents, the government of Thailand was cited by 6 percent, and the local population was cited by only 3 percent. This suggests that the local community—regardless of whether it supports or opposes the DSEZ—feels little agency over the project's execution and little responsibility for its success or failure.

Although the analysis up to this point has shown survey responses that tended to be more negative of the DSEZ than positive, the respondents were inclined to fix the project's shortcomings rather than abandon it altogether. Only 21 of 250 respondents (8 percent) recommended terminating the project (Figure 5.9). The largest group of respondents (22 percent) wanted (in the words of the survey questionnaire) to "thoroughly reevaluate the design of the project and its impacts on local communities." Not far behind were those who wanted more consultation (18 percent) and more transparency (17 percent), and significant numbers also advocated higher compensation (14 percent), more hiring

Figure 5.8
Who Should Be Responsible and Accountable for This Project?

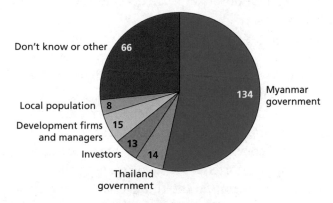

NOTE: Eight participants did not respond to this question, and they are counted in the "don't know or other" category.

Figure 5.9
Recommendations for the Dawei Project

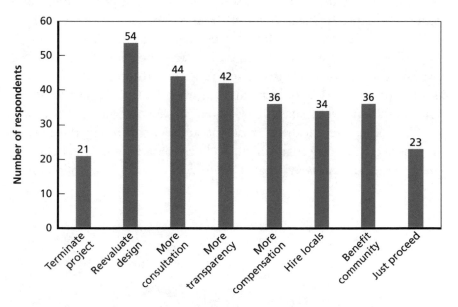

NOTE: Respondents could choose more than one recommendation.

of locals (14 percent), and more benefits to the community (14 percent). Only 23 respondents (9 percent) supported the project without significant reservations. (Respondents could choose more than one recommendation.)

The results of this survey should be taken as suggestive rather than determinative. That is, given the limited sample size and the real possibility of implicit intimidation (or merely ingrained fear of authority in a society just beginning to emerge from decades of military rule), the opinions relayed in this chapter should be understood as one set of data points rather than the definitive portrait of a community's views. But given the virtual silencing of most of Myanmar's citizens on so many issues for so many years, even a small voice can say important things.

Perhaps the most important thing that the survey respondents said is that they want to be better informed, be more meaningfully consulted, and have greater control. A majority of respondents expressed little or no familiarity with the project (see Figure 4.1 in Chapter Four), but (as the rest of the survey responses make clear) this does *not* mean that these community members were apathetic. Many of the same respondents who described themselves as unfamiliar with the project's details also expressed deep concern about the impact that it would have on their families, their livelihoods, and their communities.

These results should be treated by the stakeholders in the DSEZ project (and in other infrastructure programs throughout Myanmar) as an opportunity. The citizens most affected by the Dawei project are persuadable, and the issues they flag (fair compensation for land, more jobs for locals) are ones that could be addressed through the normal process of community engagement and negotiation. In the next chapter, we suggest some pathways that stakeholders may consider following.

CHAPTER SIX

Summary and Policy Recommendations

However the DSEZ might be serving to increase the prosperity of Myanmar as a whole, it does not seem (at least to the 250 villagers surveyed in this study) to have brought much benefit to the local communities most directly affected. A substantial majority of respondents were largely uninformed about the project and did not see it as having much impact on their lives. To the extent that they saw it as having an impact, respondents reported more negative than positive observations and expectations. Most respondents saw outsiders (particularly foreigners) as the most likely beneficiaries of the DSEZ—and themselves as the parties most likely to suffer its ill effects. The problems of the project, however, were largely seen as solvable: Fewer than 9 percent wanted to terminate the DSEZ, and an overwhelming majority favored solutions (including higher compensation for confiscated land, hiring of more locals, and increased consultation) that are amenable to negotiation. Moreover, the party responsible for such negotiations—and for implementing any recommendations—was not in great doubt: A majority felt that the government of Myanmar should be held responsible and accountable for the project's success or failure. If the government chooses to refocus efforts, it may have an opportunity to win the community's support. The message relayed by the survey data is one of alienation and skepticism but not necessarily outright opposition (at least not yet).

Given the scope of the project, the drastic impact it will have on the region, and the local population's sentiment that the central government bears ultimate responsibility for the DSEZ, Myanmar's government should ensure that the developers establish clear avenues for communication and cooperation with the local communities. This may be easier said than done: Since the military coup of General Ne Win in 1962, Myanmar has been governed by the centralized diktats of a series of military rulers. Grassroots community engagement has been seen as a threat to the established order, not a governing technique to be actively encouraged. Even the basic mechanics of electoral democracy have been viewed by the military as inconvenient exercises at best. The election of 1990, in which Aung San Suu Kyi's National League for Democracy won an overwhelming victory, was never honored by the junta. An election held in 2010 was boycotted by the National League for Democracy, but the general election of 2015 brought the party and Aung San Suu Kyi into power as partners of the military. Under the nation's constitution, one-fourth of the seats in parliament are reserved for the military—enough, under the document's carefully structured balance, to provide an ironclad veto.

If the central government decides to embark on a course of grassroots engagement, it will have to better inform the villagers about the project's goals, timetables, and potential impacts on local communities. The lack of strong informational outreach will create (or perpetuate) uncertainty about the future among the villagers, will deprive them of an opportunity to assess and cope with possible changes to their livelihoods, and will degrade their right to advocate for their interests. Furthermore, leaving local communities with no clear knowledge about the project or sense of agency in their own lives may result in rapid growth in discontent and opposition, negative global publicity, and conceivably even security challenges to the project.

Giving the local populations and their self-selected advocates a voice, however, is only a first step. Instead of merely providing window dressing for decisions made elsewhere, the communities should be better integrated into the decisionmaking process. The issues raised by survey respondents are likely to be at the top of any community-involvement agenda—including, most notably, the following:

- Relocation should be voluntary rather than forced, with compensation for any land appropriated given at levels that the stakeholders regard as fair. Of all the issues raised by survey respondents, concerns about relocation and unfair compensation for land ranked the highest.

- To the maximum extent possible, local workers should be offered jobs (particularly those not requiring specialized training) ahead of applicants from outside the communities.
- Any negative impact on the health, safety, or cultural integrity of the community should be discussed in advance with the local residents, with a view toward enlisting them as partners in crafting less-disruptive solutions.

People who live in the areas adjacent to the project should have confidence that, although they may have to sacrifice the most in accommodating the DSEZ, they will also be among the effort's principal beneficiaries. If the local population perceives itself as suffering harm for the benefit of foreigners or the central government, it is possible that residents could find ways to undermine, or even covertly sabotage, the effort.[1] Failure to adequately compensate those giving up their farmlands, perhaps more than any other concrete effect, will fuel long-term grievances; this type of dislocation could have a devastating impact on families struggling in an increasingly expensive and industrialized area. Even if the project enriches a portion of the local population, it could drive up overall poverty and downgrade public well-being. Compensation formulas should be transparent and account for the land appreciation and families' unwanted transitions.

The specific demands and proposals put forward by the communities may differ from those listed in this report. Thus, the meaningful involvement of the villagers themselves—and their genuine and

---

[1]   The extent of sabotage is difficult to determine, given the lack of accessibility that the government of Myanmar and local authorities give to independent journalists and nongovernmental organizations. A typical example of sabotage is the case of Saw O Moo, an indigenous Karen activist who led community protests demanding preservation of forests on which villagers depended for their economic support. In April 2018, he was killed, reportedly by government troops. Military authorities said that he was "suspected of sabotage." See Jonathan Watts, "Indigenous Environmental Campaigner Killed by Myanmar Government," *The Guardian*, April 13, 2018.

trusted advocates—is fundamentally important for any stable and lasting solution. Although consultations and a firm commitment to transparency may entail additional challenges, they will also ensure that the surrounding communities are more likely to act as supporters and facilitators of DSEZ investments and are willing to withstand some of the unanticipated problems and contribute to the project's success.

As Myanmar works to develop its infrastructure, it is in the ultimate interest of the central and regional governments to partner more effectively with local communities. To ensure the success of plans like the DSEZ, the people who are forced to alter their lives and livelihoods to accommodate such efforts must be—and must *feel* themselves to be—true beneficiaries of these projects.

A Point on Methodology

Very little opinion survey work has been conducted in Myanmar, largely because of the inherent difficulties of eliciting public opinion in a nation just emerging from more than half a century of military rule. The infrastructure of civil society (including groups with long-standing experience in survey work) is in its infancy. Most Burmese citizens, quite reasonably, are somewhat guarded in offering their opinions on potentially sensitive topics—particularly to strangers whose agendas they may not fully trust. This report is presented with all of these caveats in mind.

In this appendix, we want to further discuss one important point about our methodology: the fact that more than half of the survey respondents described themselves as "not at all familiar" with the DSEZ, yet they expressed a full range of opinions about it and were therefore included in the data set.

Of the survey's 250 respondents, 145 described themselves as "not at all familiar" with the Dawei project. The other 105 expressed at least some familiarity (this group included two respondents who answered "don't know"). This raises a methodological question: Should the respondents who said that they had no familiarity with the project be excluded from the data set? We included the data from these respondents in this report for the following reasons:

- This survey is a measure of the *opinions* of the community members living near the DSEZ. It is not a measure of only the community members who had significant knowledge of the project. Indeed, such a definition would require the researchers not simply to rely on self-selection (i.e., respondents' own assessment of their knowledge) but instead to make arbitrary decisions about which respondents truly were or were not knowledgeable.

- The respondents who described themselves as "not at all familiar" with the project nonetheless had very definite opinions about it. Of the opportunities to provide a response of "don't know" rather than a scored response to a survey question, the respondents who claimed to be unfamiliar with the DSEZ answered "don't know" 7 percent of the time, compared with 6 percent for respondents claiming greater familiarity.

- The opinions expressed by the not-familiar respondents did not appear to differ notably from the opinions of those reporting greater familiarity (see the comparison later in this appendix).

- A significant percentage of those describing themselves as not familiar (14 percent) actually *were* verifiably familiar with the DSEZ. Thirteen of these respondents had worked on the project (compared with 20, or 19 percent, of those who described themselves as more familiar). Seven others reported the specific impact on their families of forced labor (one respondent), intimidation (two respondents), or food insecurity (five respondents, including one who also reported intimidation); seven members of the more-familiar group reported the same experiences (two forced labor, two intimidation, three food insecurity). Moreover, an additional 39 respondents (compared with 25 in the more-familiar group) provided specific comments or recommendations in the unstructured part of the interview. In all, 41 percent of the "not at all familiar" respondents (compared with 50 percent of the more-familiar group, by the same metrics) displayed at least some familiarity with the project.

Those Describing Themselves as "Not at All Familiar" Were Only Marginally Less Likely to Express Opinions About the Project

There were 37 questions that permitted a scoring of "don't know" or meaningful nonresponse (that is, questions excluding unstructured sections and questions providing purely factual material about the respondent's background). An additional six questions were less structured but permitted respondents to refrain from providing a reply.

Those in the not-familiar category (145 respondents) provided 475 responses of "don't know" to the 37 structured questions, for an overall rate of 9 percent. When the 335 nonresponses to unstructured questions are factored in, either the response was "don't know" or no reply was offered 13 percent of the time.

Those in the more-familiar category (105 respondents) provided 285 responses of "don't know" to the 37 structured questions, for an overall rate of 7 percent. When the 214 nonresponses to unstructured questions are factored in, either the response was "don't know" or no reply was offered 11 percent of the time.

In brief, respondents who described themselves as wholly unfamiliar with the project were only slightly less likely to provide opinions about all aspects of it.

The Opinions Expressed by the Not-Familiar Group Tracked Relatively Closely to Those of the More-Familiar Group

To determine how excluding the not-familiar group might affect the overall results, we recalculated several of the key charts for comparison. The results show a close degree of correspondence, regardless of whether the data set includes the entire group of 250 respondents, the 105 respondents who expressed some degree of familiarity, or even just the 145 respondents who described themselves as "not at all familiar" with the project. See Figures A.1 through A.4.

Figure A.1
How Has the Dawei Project Affected the Local Employment Situation?

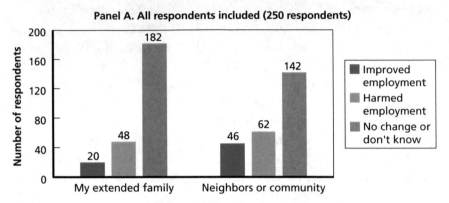

Panel A. All respondents included (250 respondents)

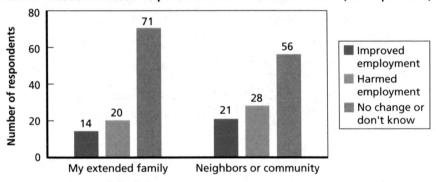

Panel B. "Not at all familiar" respondents excluded from the data set (105 respondents)

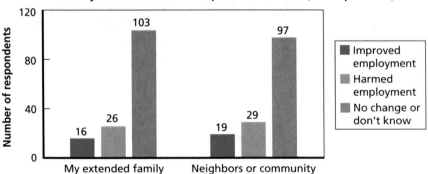

Panel C. Only "not at all familiar" respondents included (145 respondents)

Figure A.2
How Has the Project Affected Local Health Outcomes?

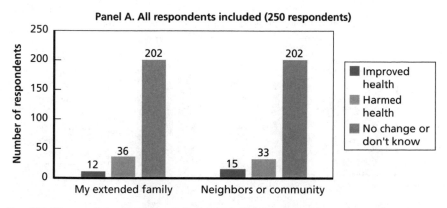

Panel A. All respondents included (250 respondents)

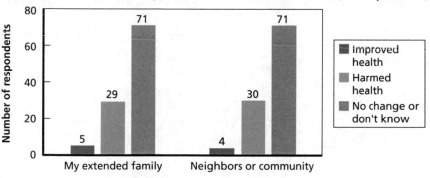

Panel B. "Not at all familiar" respondents excluded from the data set (105 respondents)

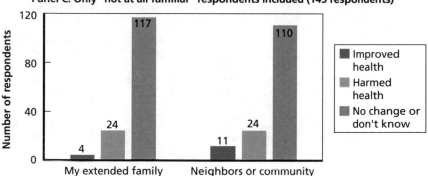

Panel C. Only "not at all familiar" respondents included (145 respondents)

Figure A.3
How Do You Think the Project Will Benefit Your Family, the Community, and Myanmar in the Long Term?

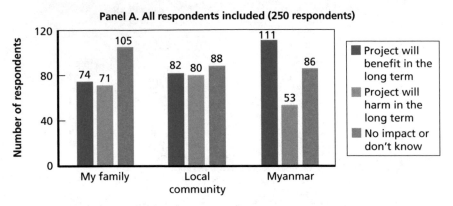

Panel A. All respondents included (250 respondents)

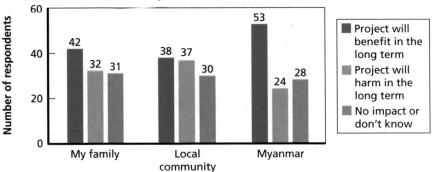

Panel B. "Not at all familiar" respondents excluded from the data set (105 respondents)

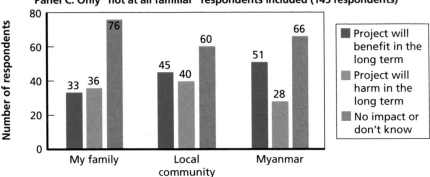

Panel C. Only "not at all familiar" respondents included (145 respondents)

Figure A.4
Who Should Be Responsible and Accountable for This Project?

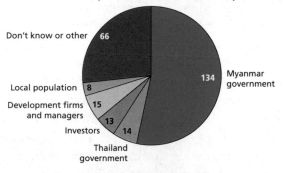

Panel A. All respondents included (250 respondents)

Don't know or other 66

Local population 8

Development firms and managers 15

Investors 13

14

Thailand government

Myanmar government 134

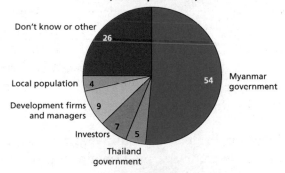

Panel B. "Not at all familiar" respondents excluded from the data set (105 respondents)

Don't know or other 26

Local population 4

Development firms and managers 9

Investors 7

5

Thailand government

Myanmar government 54

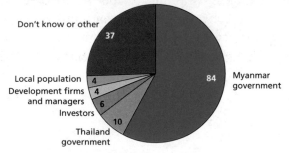

Panel C. Only "not at all familiar" respondents included (145 respondents)

Don't know or other 37

Local population 4

Development firms and managers 4

Investors 6

10

Thailand government

Myanmar government 84

NOTE: Eight participants did not respond to this question, and such partici-pants are counted in the "don't know or other" category in each panel.

How to Interpret the Response of "Not at All Familiar"

Why did a majority of the survey respondents describe themselves as "not at all familiar" with the Dawei project and then go on to demonstrate themselves to be almost as familiar as the rest of the survey respondents? Each of the 145 respondents might have had a different rationale, but two possibilities seem particularly worthy of note:

- Many respondents were likely to have viewed an outside survey team with some low-grade suspicion and initially sought to downplay their level of familiarity. In Myanmar, speaking one's mind—particularly to strangers—is not always a risk-free endeavor.
- Different respondents with similar levels of familiarity may have answered the same survey questions differently. For the large majority of respondents who had not directly worked on the DSEZ project—87 percent of the data set—a reply of "not at all familiar" might have been effectively interchangeable with one of "somewhat familiar," "moderately familiar," "familiar," or even (for individuals with particularly high self-confidence) "very familiar." The response may have less to do with an individual's actual familiarity than with his or her degree of self-assurance.

As the discussion in this appendix suggests, excluding these respondents from the data universe might not have generated very different results. For a variety of reasons, however, it would likely have represented a less complete sampling, and one probably less representative of the very real apprehensions in the community—apprehensions not only about the project itself but also about government authorities, outsiders, and the changes rapidly rolling over Burmese society.

References

"An Industrial Project That Could Change Myanmar," *International Herald Tribune: The Global Edition of the New York Times*, November 26, 2010. As of December 14, 2017:
http://www.nytimes.com/2010/11/27/world/asia/27iht-myanmar.html

Aung, Zaw, "Dawei Special Economic Zone: Its Prospects and Challenges," paper presented at the 4th International Conference on Human Rights and Human Development, Chulalongkorn University, Thailand, August 18–19, 2011. As of December 14, 2017:
https://www.scribd.com/doc/95726953/
Dawei-Special-Economic-Zone-Its-Prospects-and-Challenges

Blank, Jonah, "India's Engagement with Myanmar: Regional Security Implications of Acting East Slowly," in Karen Stoll Farrell and Šumit Ganguly, eds., *Heading East: Security, Trade, and Environment Between India and Southeast Asia*, New Delhi: Oxford University Press, 2016, pp. 69–89.

Blank, Jonah, Jennifer D. P. Moroney, Angel Rabasa, and Bonny Lin, *Look East, Cross Black Waters: India's Interest in Southeast Asia*, Santa Monica, Calif.: RAND Corporation, RR-1021-AF, 2015. As of February 4, 2019:
https://www.rand.org/pubs/research_reports/RR1021.html

Central Intelligence Agency, *The World Factbook: Burma*, accessed November 6, 2018. As of February 4, 2019:
https://www.cia.gov/library/publications/the-world-factbook/geos/bm.html

Chantavanich, S., and P. Vungsiriphisal, "Myanmar Migrants to Thailand: Economic Analysis and Implications to Myanmar Development," in Hank Lim and Yasuhiro Yamada, eds., *Economic Reforms in Myanmar: Pathways and Prospects*, Bangkok: Bangkok Research Center, Research Report No. 10, IDE-JETRO, 2013, pp. 213–280.

Dawei Development Association, *Voices from the Ground: Concerns over the Dawei Special Economic Zone and Related Projects*, Dawei, Myanmar, September 2014. As of May 20, 2018:
https://earthrights.org/wp-content/uploads/
voice_from_the_ground_eng_online.compressed.pdf

DDA—*See* Dawei Development Association.

Geary, K., *"Our Land, Our Lives": Time Out on the Global Land Rush*, Oxford, UK: Oxfam International, Briefing Note, October 2012. As of May 21, 2018: https://www.oxfam.org/sites/www.oxfam.org/files/ bn-land-lives-freeze-041012-en_1.pdf

Htun, Theingi, "Dawei SEZ Project Sparks Hopes and Worries," *Mizzima*, January 25, 2016. As of December 14, 2017: http://www.mizzima.com/business-features/ dawei-sez-project-sparks-hopes-and-worries

Human Rights Watch, *"The Farmer Becomes the Criminal": Land Confiscation in Burma's Karen State*, New York, November 2016. As of May 21, 2018: https://www.hrw.org/sites/default/files/report_pdf/burma1116_web_0.pdf

Jagan, Larry, "Myanmar Renews SEZ Push," *Bangkok Post*, October 2, 2017.

Kugelman, Michael, and Susan L. Levenstein, eds., *The Global Farms Race: Land Grabs, Agricultural Investment, and the Scramble for Food Security*, Washington, D.C.: Island Press, 2013.

Marks, Danny, and Tammy Chou, "It's Time to Scrap the Dawei Special Economic Zone," *Frontier Myanmar*, August 29, 2017. As of May 20, 2018: https://frontiermyanmar.net/en/its-time-to-scrap-the-dawei-special-economic-zone

Mon, Kyaw Hsu, "In Dawei, ITD Projects Suspended, Not Terminated: Minister," *The Irrawaddy*, December 3, 2013. As of January 11, 2018: http://www.irrawaddy.com/business/ dawei-itd-projects-suspended-terminated-minister.html

"Myanmar Sets $2.80 Daily Minimum Wage in Bid to Boost Investment," Reuters, August 29, 2015. As of November 6, 2018: https://www.reuters.com/article/ us-myanmar-economy-wages-idUSKCN0QY0A620150829

Myint-U, Thant, *Where China Meets India: Burma and the New Crossroads of Asia*, New York: Farrar, Straus and Giroux, 2011.

O'Connor, Brennan, "Myanmar: The Dawei Special Economic Zone: Amid Delays, Local Opposition to the Project Is Growing," *The Diplomat*, April 11, 2016. As of January 10, 2018: https://thediplomat.com/2016/04/myanmar-the-dawei-special-economic-zone/

Otto, Ben, "Rohingya Camps in Bangladesh Start to Look Permanent," *Wall Street Journal*, April 3, 2018. As of May 20, 2018: https://www.wsj.com/articles/ rohingya-camps-in-bangladesh-start-to-look-permanent-1522762656

Panu Wongcha-um, "Split Visions of Dawei's Future as Thailand, Myanmar Restart Special Economic Zone Project," *Channel News Asia*, May 25, 2017. As of December 12, 2017:
http://www.channelnewsasia.com/news/asiapacific/
split-visions-of-dawei-s-future-as-thailand-myanmar-restart-8883366

Pearce, Fred, *The Land Grabbers: The New Fight over Who Owns the Earth*, Boston, Mass.: Beacon Press, 2012.

Roberts, Paul, *The End of Food: The Coming Crisis in the World Food Industry*, New York: Mariner Books, 2009.

Szep, Jason, and Amy Sawitta Lefevre, "Japan, Thailand Race to Rescue Myanmar's Struggling Dawei," Reuters, September 21, 2012. As of January 11, 2018:
https://www.reuters.com/article/us-myanmar-thailand-dawei/
exclusive-japan-thailand-race-to-rescue-of-myanmars-struggling-dawei-
idUSBRE88K0D920120921

"Thailand, Myanmar to Revive South-East Asia's Largest Industrial Zone in 2015," *Straits Times*, December 4, 2014. As of May 20, 2018:
http://www.straitstimes.com/asia/se-asia/
thailand-myanmar-to-revive-south-east-asias-largest-industrial-zone-in-2015

Thein, Myat, *Economic Development of Myanmar*, Singapore: Institute of Southeast Asian Studies, 2004.

Toe Lwin, Ei Ei, "Dawei SEZ Sparks Concern amid Promises," *Myanmar Times*, December 3, 2012. As of January 11, 2018:
https://www.mmtimes.com/national-news/
3450-dawei-sez-sparks-concern-amid-promises.html

———, "Civil Society Group Calls for Freeze on Dawei Economic Zone," *Myanmar Times*, October 13, 2014. As of January 11, 2018:
https://www.mmtimes.com/business/
11919-civil-society-group-calls-for-freeze-on-dawei-economic-zone.html

United States Code, Title 22, Chapter 32, Section 2304, Human Rights and Security Assistance.

Watts, Jonathan, "Indigenous Environmental Campaigner Killed by Myanmar Government," *The Guardian*, April 13, 2018. As of May 21, 2018:
https://www.theguardian.com/environment/2018/apr/13/
indigenous-environmental-campaigner-saw-o-moo-killed-by-myanmar-
government-karen-state

Win, Su Phyo, "Two New Taskforces to Monitor and Facilitate Dawei SEZ," *Myanmar Times*, September 28, 2017. As of December 14, 2017:
https://www.mmtimes.com/news/
two-new-taskforces-monitor-and-facilitate-dawei-sez.html

World Bank, "Country Score Card: Myanmar 2014," Logistics Performance Index, 2014. As of December 14, 2017:
https://lpi.worldbank.org/international/scorecard/line/200/C/MMR/2014

Xe, "Currency Converter," web tool, accessed November 6, 2018. As of February 4, 2019:
https://www.xe.com/currencyconverter/convert/
?Amount=3%2C600%2C000&From=MMK&To=USD

Zegema, B., *Land and Power: The Growing Scandal Surrounding the New Wave of Investments in Land*, Oxford, UK: Oxfam International, Oxfam Briefing Paper 151, September 22, 2001. As of May 21, 2018:
https://www.oxfam.org/sites/www.oxfam.org/files/
bp151-land-power-rights-acquisitions-220911-en.pdf

About the Authors

Jonah Blank is a senior political scientist at the RAND Corporation and author of *Arrow of the Blue-Skinned God: Retracing the Ramayana Through India* and *Mullahs on the Mainframe: Islam and Modernity Among the Daudi Bohras*. He formerly served as policy director for South and Southeast Asia on the staff of the Senate Foreign Relations Committee and is currently based in Indonesia. He holds a Ph.D. in anthropology.

Shira Efron is a policy researcher at the RAND Corporation and a professor at the Pardee RAND Graduate School. She works primarily on issues related to Israel, the Middle East, and food security in the Middle East and Africa. She holds a Ph.D. in policy analysis.

Katya Migacheva is an associate behavioral and social scientist at the RAND Corporation, where she has studied religion and conflict, challenges in societies undergoing transition, hate speech and hate crime, countering violent extremism, and school transformation. She holds a Ph.D. in social psychology.